Money and You

Peter Rader

PICTURE CREDITS

Cover © Randy Faris/Corbis; title page, pages 5 (top left), 17, 23 (bottom right), 26 (top right), 28 (top inset), 30 (bottom right), 31 (top left & right), 32, 34-b, 34-e, 35-b, 35-f, 36 © Corbis; pages 2-3 © Joos Mind/Getty Images; pages 4 (top), 6 (U.S. bills insert), 30 (top left), 34-f Cathy Melloan; pages 5 (bottom left), 26 (bottom right) © Digital Vision/Getty Images; pages 5 (right), 25 (bottom right), 34-a © Chip Henderson/ Index Stock Imagery; page 6 © Premium Stock/Corbis; pages 8, 10 (left), 25 (top left) © The Granger Collection, New York; page 9 (right) © Brandon D. Cole/ Corbis; page 9 (left) © Bob Krist/Corbis; page 10 (top right) © Jonathan Blair/Corbis; page 10 (bottom right) © Giraudon/Art Resource, NY; page 11 (top) © James Leynse/ Corbis; page 11 (bottom) © Brian Hagiwara/Getty Images; pages 13, 14 (left), 25 (bottom left), 25 (top right) © Michael Krasowitz/Getty Images; page 14 (center) © Adrian Weinbrecht/Getty Images; page 14 (right), 34-c © SW Productions/Getty Images; page 15 © Tom Stewart/Corbis; pages 16, 19-22, 35-c, 35-d, 35-e Photography by Karen Ballard; page 18 (left) © Thinkstock/Getty Images; page 18 (center) © A.Inden/Corbis; page 18 (right) © Darama/Corbis; page 23 (top) © William Manning/Corbis; pages 23 (bottom left), page 30 (bottom left) © C Squared Studios/Getty Images; page 26 (left) © Julie Toy/Getty Images; pages 27, 31 (center right) © James Leynse/Corbis; page 28 (bottom left) © Reuters/Corbis; page 28 (bottom center) © Phil Schermeister/Corbis; page 28 (bottom right) © Layne Kennedy/ Corbis; page 29 (top) © Bettmann/Corbis; page 30 (top right) © Ed Bock/Corbis; page 31 (center left) © Alen MacWeeney/Corbis; page 33 (left) *Kids Are Consumers* by Marita Garey, © 2002 National Geographic Society, photos (foreground, clockwise from top left) © Spencer Grant/PhotoEdit, © Claude Guillaumin/Stone, © Howard Kingsnorth/ Stone, © Ian Royd/Image Bank, (background, left to right) © Michael Newman/PhotoEdit,

© Chuck Savage/The Stock Market; page 33 (center) *Kids Manage Money* by Ellen Keller, © 2002 National Geographic Society, photos (foreground, clockwise from top left) © Mugshots/The Stock Market, © Lloyd Wolf Photography, © John Terence Turner/ FPG, (background, left to right) © Stephen Frisch/Stock Boston, © Bob Daemmrich/ Stock Boston; page 33 (right) *Dust Bowl Days* by Kate Connell, © 2002 National Geographic Society, photo © Western History Collection, University of Oklahoma Library; page 34-d © Thomas Del Brase/Getty Images; page 35-a © John Turner/Corbis.

Produced through the worldwide resources of the National Geographic Society, John M. Fahey, Jr., President and Chief Executive Officer; Gilbert M. Grosvenor, Chairman of the Board; Nina D. Hoffman, Executive Vice President and President, Books and Education Publishing Group.

PREPARED BY NATIONAL GEOGRAPHIC SCHOOL PUBLISHING

Ericka Markman, Senior Vice President and President, Children's Books and Education Publishing Group; Steve Mico, Senior Vice President, Editorial Director, Publisher; Francis Downey, Executive Editor; Richard Easby, Editorial Manager; Anne Stone, Lori Dibble Collins Editors; Bea Jackson, Director of Layout and Design; Jim Hiscott, Design Manager; Cynthia Olson, Art Director; Margaret Sidlosky, Illustrations Director; Matt Wascavage, Manager of Publishing Services; Sean Philpotts, Jane Ponton, Production Managers; Ted Tucker, Production Specialist.

MANUFACTURING AND QUALITY CONTROL

Christopher A. Liedel, Chief Financial Officer; Phillip L. Schlosser, Director; Clifton M. Brown III, Manager.

◄ **A shopper saves money by checking prices.**

Contents

CONSULTANT AND REVIEWER
Jody Giblin, Vice President, Finance and Operations,
National Geographic Society

BOOK DESIGN/PHOTO RESEARCH
Steve Curtis Design, Inc.

Published by the National Geographic Society
1145 17th Street N.W.
Washington, D.C. 20036-4688

ISBN-13: 978-0-7922-5450-8
ISBN-10: 0-7922-5450-3

2012
2 3 4 5 6 7 8 9 10 11 12 13 14 15

Printed in Canada.

Thinking About Money

People think a lot about money. We think about ways to earn money. We think about ways to spend money. We think about ways to save it, too.

Money helps us buy the things we need or want. It helps us pay for food, a home, and clothing. It lets us pay for movies, games, and fun. Money helps us live. What else does money do?

▲ **Earning money**

▲ **Spending money**

▲ **Saving money**

5

Big Idea
Money helps people buy the things they need or want.

Set Purpose
Read to learn about the different ways people use money.

Questions You Will Explore

What is the history of money?

What are the best ways to save money?

The Story of Money

Money comes in many sizes and shapes.
It comes in many colors and designs.
Each country has its own money.
Different kinds of money are worth
different amounts. In this book, you will
learn the story of money.

◀ **Money looks different
around the world.**

▲ People long ago traded with one
another instead of using money.

Trading for Goods

Long ago, people did not need money. They
hunted for food. They built their own shelters.
They made clothes from animal skins.

Sometimes people wanted things they did not
have. They traded with other people to get
these things. For example, if they had extra
food, they traded it for cloth or other goods.

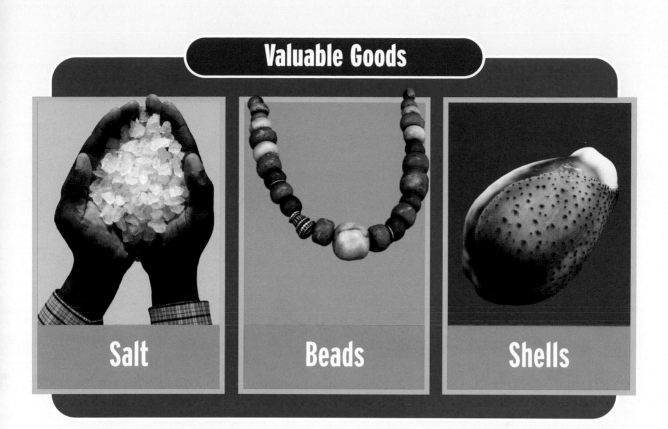

Valuable Goods

Salt

Beads

Shells

Paying with Goods

Goods that were hard to find were valuable.
People started using these goods as money.
For example, some people paid with salt.
Some people used beads or shells.

Buying and selling this way was not easy.
The goods were hard to carry. They took up
too much space. People needed a better way
to buy and sell.

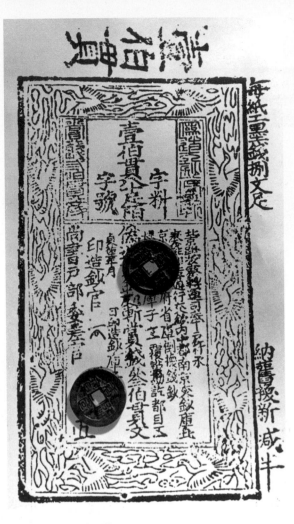

▲ This is early Chinese paper money and coins.

▲ These are some early coins.

Early Money

Soon, people had a better idea. They began making **coins.** They made coins out of metals such as gold and silver. Large coins had more metal. They were worth more. Small coins had less metal and were worth less. Later, the Chinese invented the first paper money. It was easier to carry than coins. But coins lasted longer.

coin — a piece of money made of metal

▲ Bills are printed in sheets and checked for flaws.

American Money

Today, Americans use both paper money and coins. Paper money is sometimes called bills. Together, coins and bills are called **cash**. The federal government makes all the country's cash. Coins come from the United States Mint. Bills come from the Bureau of Engraving and Printing. The government says how much the money is worth.

cash — coins and paper money

▶ Coins and paper money are called cash.

How a Check Works

Pretend you have $400 in the bank. You want to buy a bike that costs $250. So you write a check.

The store takes your check to the bank and turns it in for cash. Now you have $150 left in the bank.

Your name and address

The person or store you are paying

Today's date

100

Chris Jeffries
123 Main Street
Alexandria, Virginia 12345

DATE _April 3rd, 2006_

PAY TO THE ORDER OF _Ike and Mike's Bikes and Trikes_ $ | 250.00 |

Two hundred fifty and ——————————— 00/100 DOLLARS

MEMO _New bike_

The amount of money you are paying

Chris Jeffries

Your signature

Checks Are Like Cash

Cash is not the only way people pay for goods and services. People also write **checks.**

Checks are almost like cash. Pretend that you have money in the bank. A check tells the bank to use that money to pay for something you buy.

People send checks in the mail. They also use checks when they do not want to carry cash.

check — a written order that tells the bank to pay a certain amount of money

12

▲ A credit card lets this woman
pay without cash.

Credit Cards

Sometimes people pay with **credit cards.** Credit
cards let you order by phone or over the
Internet. You can also use a credit card when
you do not have cash.

How does it work? You give your credit card
number to a store. Your credit card company
pays the store now. You pay the company back
later. The company charges you a little bit for
using the card.

credit card — a card that lets you buy something now
but pay for it later

13

Things You Budget For

Things you need

Things you want

Future needs and wants

A Money Plan

People need to be careful with their money.
They need a plan for using it. This plan is called
a **budget.** A budget includes things you need,
such as food and clothing. It includes things you
want, such as movies. It also includes planning
for the future. A budget helps people know how
much money they can spend. It says how much
they should save.

....
budget — a plan for using money

▲ Money adds up in
the bank.

Saving Money

One way to save money is to put it in
a **bank.** Banks help people take care
of their money until they need it.

Banks pay you **interest** for saving
money in the bank. The more money
you save, the more interest you earn.
So banks help you earn money.

....

bank — a place to keep money

interest — the money that a bank pays people for
saving in a bank

Stop and Think!

What are the different
ways people use money?

Recap
Explain the different
ways that people
use money.

Set Purpose
Read about three
students with plans
for their money.

Money Lesson

Meet Jake, Nina, and TeShawn. They are students at Robinson Secondary School. These kids are learning an important lesson about money. They are learning how to save.

Making a Plan

Jake wants to buy a new soccer ball and new soccer shoes. Nina and TeShawn want to go on a class trip. These things cost money.

The kids make a plan. They will earn money by doing small jobs. Jake can rake leaves. Nina can take care of her little sister. TeShawn will walk his neighbor's dog.

Ways Kids Earn Money

Raking leaves

Babysitting

Taking care of animals

Setting a Monthly Goal

Jake, Nina, and TeShawn have a goal. They each want to save $10 a month. The kids decide to put their money in a bank. They choose the bank at school. It is run by students. TeShawn works at the bank. He is a **teller.** A teller counts people's money.

....
teller — a person who works behind the counter in a bank

▼ **TeShawn is a teller at the school bank.**

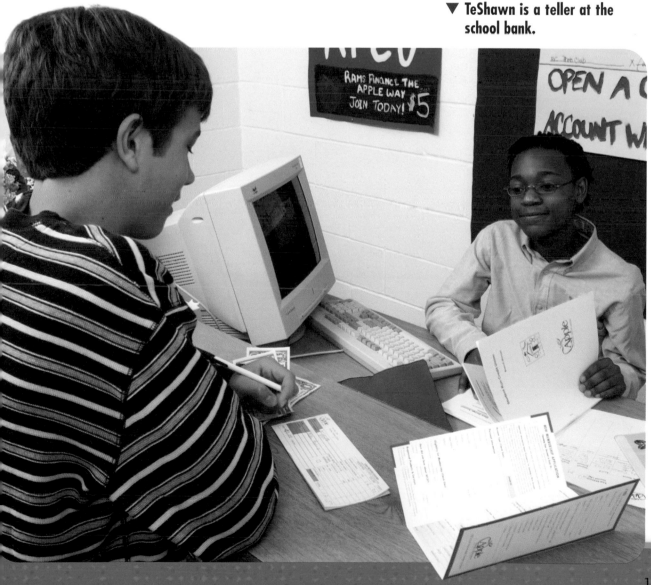

Opening an Account

TeShawn helps Jake and Nina open new **bank accounts.** A bank account is a place to store money in the bank. Each account is private. Each has a different number.

The kids want to save money. So they open savings accounts. What if they wanted to spend the money right away? They would open checking accounts.

....
bank account — a private place to store money in the bank

▼ **TeShawn helps Nina manage her money.**

Deposits and Withdrawals

Today Jake, Nina, and TeShawn put money into the bank. This is called a **deposit**. To make a deposit, the kids fill out special slips of paper. On the slips, they write their names and account numbers.

Someday the kids will want to use their money. They will take it out of the bank. This is called making a **withdrawal**.

....

deposit — an amount of money put into a bank account

withdrawal — an amount of money taken out of a bank account

▲ Jake and Nina have money to deposit in the bank.

▼ Nina's deposit slip

Apple FEDERAL CREDIT UNION	P.O. Box 1200 Fairfax, Virginia 22030		CASH RECEIVED VOUCHER CHECKS CREDITED SUBJECT TO COLLECTION		
			DESCRIPTION	DOLLARS	CENTS
			SHARES (SAVINGS) -000	10	00
DATE	September 12, 2006		SHARE DRAFTS (CHECKING) -017		
ACCOUNT NUMBER	123000543-12		MONEY MARKET -015		
		CHECK HERE IF NEW ADDRESS	HOLIDAY CLUB -060		
NAME	Nina Smith		VACATION CLUB -065		
ADDRESS	123 Main Street		IRA - YEAR _____		
		☐	LOAN # _____		
			LOAN # _____		
			CERTIFICATE # _____		
CASH ☑ _____	CHECKS _____		RECEIVED BY		
			TOTAL	10	00

AFCU-17

Keeping Records

Banks keep careful records. They keep track of people's deposits and withdrawals. Every month, the bank sends a **statement.** The statement tells the kids how much money is in their accounts. It also tells how much interest the bank has paid to the kids.

statement — a written record of how much money is in a bank account

▼ Nina and Jake just got their bank statements.

Seeing Results

Jake, Nina, and TeShawn look at their bank statements. They like seeing how much money they have saved. They are happy about the interest they have earned.

Soon Jake will be able to pay for the soccer ball and shoes. Soon Nina and TeShawn will go on their class trip. They will see the results of their hard work.

Stop and Think!

HOW will the three kids meet their goals?

▼ Nina and TeShawn will send postcards home from their trip.

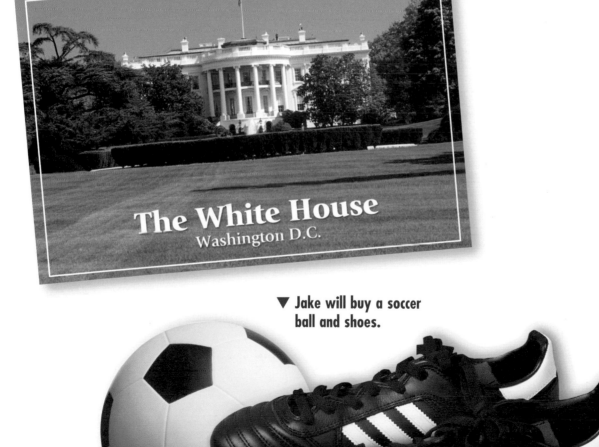

The White House
Washington D.C.

▼ Jake will buy a soccer ball and shoes.

Recap
Describe how Jake, Nina, and TeShawn plan to reach their goals.

Set Purpose
Read more about money and its many forms.

CONNECT WHAT YOU HAVE LEARNED

Money and You

Money is important. It helps us buy the things we want or need. We need to make careful choices about how we use our money.

Here are some ideas that you learned about money.

- Long ago, people traded for items they wanted or needed.
- Today, people use coins, paper money, checks, and credit cards.
- A budget helps people decide how to use their money.
- Banks are places where people keep their money safe until they need it.

Check What You Have Learned

HOW do people pay for what they want or need?

▲ People traded for goods long ago.

▲ A credit card lets a person pay without cash.

▲ People set a budget to make sure they can buy what they need.

▲ Banks help people save their money.

Starting a Business

Do you want some extra cash? Maybe you can start your own business. There are lots of things you can do. You can sell arts and crafts that you have made. You can wash a neighbor's car. You can mow lawns. What else can you do to earn money? Find something that you like to do. Then turn it into cash.

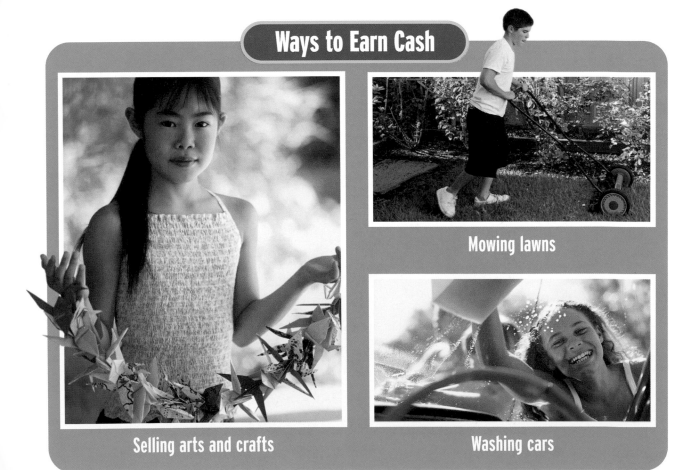

Ways to Earn Cash

Mowing lawns

Selling arts and crafts

Washing cars

▲ Take a close look at bills to see how they are made.

Fake Money

There are laws against making fake money. People go to jail if they are caught. But some people still try to print their own money. Making fake money is not as easy as it seems. Paper money has a thread that glows under a special light. The ink also changes color when the bill is moved. And the paper has a special design called a watermark. You can see the watermark by holding a bill up to a light. These features make it hard to print a fake bill.

Making Coins

All our coins are made by the United States Mint. Coins start as large metal sheets. A machine cuts the metal into small circles. Then the circles are heated and stamped with a design.

The Mint has two buildings for making coins. How can you tell which building a coin is from? Look for a small letter on the coin. "D" means it was made in Denver. "P" means it was made in Philadelphia.

▲ A coin minted in Denver

▲ The buffalo nickel was made between 1913 and 1938.

▲ This is a rare Indian Head gold coin from 1914.

▲ This is a silver dollar from 1804.

▲ A coin being made

What Is It Worth?

Some people collect old coins. Many old coins are rare. That means there are not many of them left. Rare coins can be worth a lot of money.

- A nickel is worth five cents. But a rare buffalo nickel can be worth up to $290,000.

- In 1914, an Indian Head gold coin was worth only $10. Today, it can be worth $350,000.

- In 1804, a silver dollar was worth $1. In 1999, that same coin sold for more than four million dollars!

Many kinds of words are used in this book. Here you will learn about words that describe. You will also learn about words that have more than one meaning.

Adjectives

An adjective is a word that describes a person, place, or thing. An adjective often goes before the word it describes. Find the adjectives below. What words do they describe?

Long ago, **large** coins were worth more than smaller ones.

Nina will take care of her **little** sister.

Jake wants to buy a **new** ball.

Banks keep **careful** records.

Multiple-Meaning Words

Some words have more than one meaning. Think about the two meanings for each of these words. Then use each word in a sentence of your own.

A man stops to **check** his watch.

Sally wrote a **check** at the store.

A man fishes from the river **bank.**

Jake saves money in the **bank.**

The bird catches a worm in its **bill.**

Luke has a $100 **bill.**

Research and Write

Write an Advertisement

You read about how people earn, spend, and save money.
Now come up with a plan for a business of your own.
What can you do to earn money?

Research
Collect books and reference materials, or go online.

Read and Take Notes
As you read, take notes and draw pictures.

Write
Create an advertisement for your new business.
Draw a picture that shows people
what the business is all about.
Describe the goods or services you
will offer. Tell people why they
should hire you, and explain how
they can contact you.

Read and Compare

Read More About Money

Find and read other books about money and its history. As you read, think about these questions.

- What can people do to make the most of their money?
- How does this help me make decisions about my money?
- What other questions do I have about money?

Books to Read

▲ Read more about saving and spending for things you want and need.

▲ Discover some ways that kids take control of their money.

▲ Learn how people managed money during hard times in the past.

Glossary

bank (page 15)
A place to keep money
Banks help people take care of their money.

bank account (page 20)
A private place to store money in the bank
Some people open a bank account so they can write checks.

budget (page 14)
A plan for using money
A budget helps people save for the future.

cash (page 11)
Coins and paper money
People often carry cash around with them.

check (page 12)
A written order that tells the bank to pay a certain amount of money
People use checks when paying by mail.

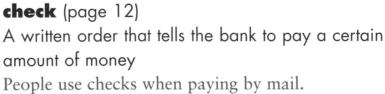

coin (page 10)
A piece of money made of metal
There are many kinds of coins in America.

credit card (page 13)
A card that lets you buy something now but pay for it later
Credit cards are useful when paying by phone.

deposit (page 21)
An amount of money put into a bank account
Banks keep track of every deposit you make.

interest (page 15)
The money that a bank pays people for saving in a bank
Interest adds to the money in your savings account.

statement (page 22)
A written record of how much money is in a bank account
Banks send a monthly statement for each account you have.

teller (page 19)
A person who works behind the counter in a bank
TeShawn is a teller at the school bank.

withdrawal (page 21)
An amount of money taken out of a bank account
You can make a withdrawal from your account when you need cash.

Index